ANGLESEY'S ISLANDS

An aerial view of Ynys Llanddwyn

First published in 2015

© Text: Margaret Hughes
Photography: J. C. Davies

Photographs are the sole copyright of:
John C. Davies
Llanfawr Lodge, Llanfawr Road, Holyhead, Anglesey LL65 2PP
Tel; 01407 762914   jcdavies@uwclub.net

ISBN: 978–1-84524-235-0

Cover design: Eleri Owen

Published by Gwasg Carreg Gwalch,
12 Iard yr Orsaf, Llanrwst Wales LL26 0EH

Tel: 01492 642031

email: books@carreg-gwalch.com
website: www.carreg-gwalch.com

Anglesey's Islands

Margaret Hughes
Photography by J. C. Davies

Tŵr Mawr on Ynys Llanddwyn

The cliffs of Ynys Cybi with South Stack

Contents

Ynys Seiriol (Puffin Island or Priestholm)

Maen y Bugail (West Mouse)

Acknowledgements . . .

As author my thanks go to the many visitors to Anglesey's islands in the past who have left written record of their experiences.

And to photographer and friend J. C. Davies for sharing his knowledge and providing such excellent pictures of some of the islands and the delights they offer. Copyright for photographs is his.

And to Geraint Hughes and Eric Lander for their enthusiastic support of the venture and to Myrddin ap Dafydd and his team for a pleasant business connection and their customary publishing skills.

Thank you, all.

Ynys Amlwch (East Mouse)

Ynys Dulas, looking towards Penmon

Ynys Moelfre

Anglesey's Islands

The island of Anglesey is itself surrounded by a necklace of islands. Some are sizeable, others merely a cluster of rocks protruding from the sea.

They proliferate along the western and northern shores where there are precipitous cliffs on the mainland. The eastern and southern shores are sandy with wide bays.

Many of these islands, large and small, have stories to tell. Remembering history, myth and legend is the purpose of this book – it is no academic treatise.

Some islands continue to make a contribution to present day life at sea and in the community. There will be a reminder of this, too.

'Anglesey's Islands' is intended to give informative pleasure, so . . . read on, and enjoy.

The Islands' 'Saints'

Many churches and chapels on Anglesey are dedicated to missionaries, Celts who are dubbed 'saints' although they were never canonised. Several of these are remembered on the surrounding islands.

Dwynwen gave her name to Ynys Llanddwyn, Gwenfaen settled at Rhoscolyn, Ffraid at Trearddur. Many of those missionaries were women.

The fifth, sixth and seventh centuries saw the arrival of Cwyfan, Cybi, Tysilio and Seiriol, all establishing their cells where they could pray and meditate in seclusion, at a time when Christianity was new to Britain. Later, churches were built on the site where their followers were welcomed, and, in two cases, monasteries too.

Why choose Anglesey, you may ask. Travelling by sea in those early days was more convenient than by land and Anglesey's islands were easier access points for those coming from Ireland, the Isle of Man, Scotland, Brittany and even from other parts of Wales.

Ynys Cwyfan, 'St Cwyfan's in the Sea' or 'Eglwys Bach y Môr'

Cross in memory of St Dwynwen, who died 25 January 465

The Anglesey pier of the Menai Suspension bridge stands on Ynys y Moch (Pigs' island)

Ynys Castell, an islet in the Strait

Ynys y Moch (Pigs' Island)

We begin our journey around Anglesey's islands at Ynys y Moch, a rocky outcrop in the Menai Strait close to the town of Porthaethwy (Menai Bridge).

These days it is difficult to imagine the Menai Strait without its two great bridges. Before 1826, when Telford's Suspension Bridge was opened to traffic, farmers and drovers sending cattle to markets on the mainland, had to persuade cattle to swim across the Strait at this, its narrowest point. This was an occupation fraught with danger, as beasts could be lost when strong currents and tides swept them down as far as Bangor or even Beaumaris, and although men in boats would give chase, beasts could be drowned. Pigs received similar treatment, although they were allowed a short respite on Ynys y Moch before continuing their hazardous journey.

In those days the annual autumn cattle market was held on land now occupied by the Antelope Hotel, on the Bangor side of the Strait. It was later moved to Porthaethwy, close to the Anglesey Arms Hotel.

A bridge had been contemplated several times before Telford's plan was accepted, but all were refused because they did not allow for the passage of ships with tall masts. Telford recognised the problem and designed his road deck to be one hundred feet above the water. At last, access and egress was made easier.

Stone for the bridge piers was quarried at Penmon and brought to the Strait in coasters. It was unloaded at the tiny islet at the east end of Porthaethwy village from where a rail had been laid down to the shore opposite Ynys y Moch, and dragged along in trucks by horses. The Anglesey pier was to be built on Ynys y Moch.

After 1826 when the bridge was opened to traffic, Porthaethwy assumed a new importance – and a new name. As 'Menai Bridge' it became a small town, a convenient stopping place for travellers using Telford's London to Holyhead road.

Ynys y Moch is now a quiet rock once more. The noise of objecting cattle is only a dream.

Ynys Gaint, an islet in the Strait linked to the Anglesey shore by a bridge

Ynys Faelog, an islet in the Strait

Two walkers cross the causeway to Ynys Tysilio

St Tysilio's church, with Britannia Bridge in the distance

Ynys Tysilio

A little to the west along the Strait from Ynys y Moch and hugging the Anglesey shore, lies Ynys Tysilio, or Church Island. Walk down the tree-lined lane which separates the bridge from the Anglesey Arms hotel and you enter another world. Traffic on the bridge is silenced.

At the foot of the hill an opening on the right leads to a pleasant promenade, the Belgian Walk, built by Flemish refugees during the First World War, to give them employment. This gives extensive views of the Strait and the bridges, ending in a causeway which is the entrance to Ynys Tysilio.

Tysilio was a missionary, the younger son of a 7th century king of Powys. Unlike his elder brother, who was aristocratic and warlike, Tysilio had a more gentle disposition, and studied under a Christian leader of his day. He came to north Wales, seeking seclusion, somewhere he could pray and meditate in peace, and found it on this small island. He set up his cell, later building a small church on the site which, in turn, was enlarged during the 15th century. A stone embedded in one wall carried the date A.D. 630. More development took place during the 19th century using much of the original stone.

The roof has three medieval trusses, the soffits of which are curved and chamfered. The windows on the north and south walls are relatively modern, but the east window is a reproduction of a 15th century window. The gable coping and a cross socket have been dated to the 15th century and the font to the 14th. 'Saint' Tysilio's church is now only used on special occasions. The parish church of St Mary, Porthaethwy, stands on the steep rise on the A5 near the Anglesey entrance to the Suspension bridge.

The island church is surrounded by an extensive graveyard, the final resting place of local inhabitants, and others, over the centuries. Servants to local wealthy families, those who died tragically at sea, all are remembered here. The graves all add to the tranquil atmosphere of the island.

From the graveyard a pathway meanders around the island shore. From here, one can look out west over the dangerous water of the Strait, to Robert Stephenson's railway bridge, originally a famous structure of iron tubes. During the 1970s a disastrous fire destroyed them, and the bridge was rebuilt, with an open rail track and a road bridge above it. This is now the A55 expressway.

Over marshland to the north of Ynys Tysilio in the nesting season, terns, shags, cormorants and gulls gather in their hundreds – a sight always popular with birdwatchers.

For many years there was a familiar sight in the Menai Strait – the school ship 'Conway' had been anchored here. She was the old man-o-war battleship 'Nile' which had changed her name with a change of use. Eventually she needed re-fit and this was to be done in Liverpool. On the day she was due to leave the Menai Strait, she went aground on the Platters rocks nearby. She began to sink. A team of workmen with oxyacetylene equipment arrived to try to save the timbers, but the ship caught fire and had to be abandoned. The Conway' sank in the Strait.

Er Cof Am : In Memory Of
JOHN HUGHES
DANIEL ROBERTS
JOHN THAYER

A laddwyd rhwng 1821 a 1822 wrth adeiladu
Pont y-Borth ac a gladdwyd
ar Llandysilio heb gofeb.
Who were killed between 1821 and 1822
during the construction of the Menai Suspension Bridge
and were buried on Church Island without a memorial.

Grŵp Telford 250 Group

A memorial in St Tysilio's church to three men who died during the construction of the Menai bridge

St Tysilio's church, with Menai Bridge in the distance

The Belgian Walk is the place to walk or rest before crossing the causeway to Ynys Tysilio

Bird watchers at a hide close to Ynys Tysilio

The pathway on Ynys Tysilio saw many onlookers on that day.

Submerged rocks and whirlpools combined with dangerous tides, make navigation through the Strait difficult, especially around the Swellies rocks which now carry a buoy to warn approaching vessels of the hazards. Sailing through here is an adventure, only to be attempted by those with the necessary knowledge. What did Tysilio make of it, we wonder.

Ynys Gorad Goch

Those approaching Anglesey over the Menai Suspension bridge in the direction of Holyhead (Caergybi) often stop in one of the two laybys on Telford's London to Holyhead (Caergybi) road to appreciate the stupendous view across the Strait to the mountains beyond. They are also attracted by the green island with its white house and tower which hugs the coast below. This is Ynys Gorad Goch (the island of the red weir).

The tidal patterns in the Menai Strait, and the rocky sea bed, make it an ideal area for weir fishing. Fish are swept into the weir when the tide is high but cannot escape. Then the fisherman comes along to retrieve his catch.

There are several weirs along the fifteen miles of the Menai Strait.

Weir fishing at Gorad Goch has provided a livelihood for many over the years.

The property is, in reality, an island divided into two by a narrow channel, now crossed by a causeway. It was originally Crown property, but passed into the hands of the Bangor Diocese, and the diocese held it for around three centuries.

While it belonged to the church, a small room in the house came to be known as The Bishop's Room where bishops of Bangor would visit to spend time in prayer and meditation. A stone embedded in the wall near the window bears the initials and date 'I.R.1808' believed to refer to one of those bishops.

In the early days fish from the weir was supplied to

A high tide partially submerges Ynys Gorad Goch

At low tide a fish weir at Ynys Gorad Goch becomes accessible to a fisherman

The Curing Tower at Ynys Gorad Goch

An angler uses his rods to secure a catch off Ynys Gorad Goch

monasteries in the area and some sold at local markets. Herring was cured in the tower.

During the 1800s the island was sold into private hands. Sometimes the property was occupied by tenants who paid a rent. Those tenants gained a livelihood by fishing the weir, and selling their catches.

When Telford's London to Holyhead road had been completed, a pathway was made through the woodland on the estate opposite the island, which made access much easier. Previously the only way had been by boat from Porthaethwy. This path led from the main road to a place on the shore opposite the island. Only a small rowing boat was needed for the crossing from there.

The Madoc Jones family, who were once tenants, lived there over three generations. Then it was regarded as an idyllic place for a home – but, was it? The three boys in the family had to go to school, and did so at the Beaumaris Grammar school. Father would row them to the shore early in the morning, they would scramble up the path to the road, walk (or run) down to Porthaethwy then catch the school bus. And the journey in reverse in the afternoon. this, five times each week.

Father would fish the weir twice a day, depending on the tides – spend time curing herring, and selling his catches. At the end of the afternoon the boys would need to be met to bring them home.

During the summer the lady of the house would have an extra chore, as she provided 'whitebait teas' for visitors. These visitors, too, would use the path to the shore where they would ring a bell fastened to a tree, to summon a boat. They would be served whitebait, brown bread and butter and a pot of tea in the Bishop's room before returning. That would be an attraction to today's tourists.

At one period a Visitors' Book was kept on the island. It showed evidence of some well known visitors, including a member of the royal family of the day, and David Lloyd George's wife and Megan, their daughter.

As one would expect from such a site, there was plenty of bird life. Writers over the years have mentioned flocks of terns, which would bombard anyone working outside. One of the Madoc Jones family would always carry a stick which he used to attack terns who attacked him. The lady gardener employed by an owner in the 1960s would always wear a strong straw hat to withstand any aerial activity. This was the lady who created a lawn at the front of the house, and surrounded it with shrubs which would withstand the foreceful weather to which Ynys Gorad Goch was subjected. And she also planted a herb garden near the tower.

Ynys Gorad Goch may appear idyllic on a pleasant summer day – but was it?

Ynys Llanddwyn

Ynys Llanddwyn (Llanddwyn Island) is on the south western tip of Anglesey, where the Irish Sea becomes the Menai Strait, has an atmosphere all its own. Be it a bright day with groups of people enjoying the spectacular views across to Caernarfon and beyond, or a dull day when it can be a lonely place, that atmosphere is present

This is because of 'saint' Dwynwen. Who was she?

Legends have developed around Dwynwen, but all describe her as 'patron saint of lovers'. One says she was Irish and walked across the Irish Sea to Anglesey to find seclusion following a disappointment in her love life. She came to search for seclusion where she could live a life of prayer and meditation. And here she could give help to others who had suffered as she had done.

The more popular story of this Celtic 'saint' is that which tells of her broken engagement to the son of Prince Maelgwn Gwynedd. When he broke off their association, God had turned him into a block of ice. In spite of her disappointment, Dwynwen had pleaded with God to bring him back to life, which God did. In gratitude, Dwynwen came to Anglesey to live a life of prayer and mediatation, and to help others who had been disappointed as she was.

Whichever legend you prefer, there is evidence that Dwynwen did, in fact, exist. The site of her cell and her early church on the island is marked with a cross.

Pilgrims came to Llanddwyn, many of them women who wished to be ensured that their lovers would be faithful.

Dwynwen's holy well was their centre of attraction.

Three modern sculptures greet the visitor to Ynys Llanddwyn

Remains of Saint Dwynwen's church, and the lighthouse seen through its window

Here women would bring crumbs of wheaten loaf which they would scatter on the water as a meal for the holy eel which lived in the well, then cover the water with a cloth. If the cloth sank into the well, they would assume that their loved ones would be unfaithful.

Today Ynys Llanddwyn is visited by thousands every year. Access is down a quiet lane from the approach to Newborough. There is a beach walk to the causeway. Visitors are warned to note the times of high tides as the causeway can be flooded and this should be remembered.

There are cottages on the island, built to house the pilots by the Caernarfon Harbour Trust, pilots who guided ships in and out of Caernarfon port and into the Menai Strait when shipping was brisk in the area.

Saint Dwynwen's church remains

Tŵr Bach, a lighthouse on Ynys Llanddwyn

The Pilots' boathouse, wedged in a cleft of land

On the shore opposite Caernarfon stand two towers. The smaller, Tŵr Bach, was built as a beacon for sailors but after a few years Tŵr Mawr was built on higher ground as sailors complained that the original tower was not easy to see from the water.

Ynys Llanddwyn once had a lifeboat station, one of the earliest to be opened in Anglesey.

Before reading about the lifeboat service, let us hear about another of Anglesey's 'saints' – Cwyfan.

The Pilots' houses on Ynys Llanddwyn

Ynys Cwyfan and the West Coast

The west coast of Anglesey is marked by a stretch of rocky islets. One of the largest is Ynys Cwyfan, north of Aberffraw. This is where the Irish Celtic 'saint' Cwyfan found tranquility, creating his cell here in the 7th century. A church was later built on the site, and this incorporated some of the original stone. A graveyard developed around it.

Access to the island has always depended on the tide. When high water made access impossible, the parson would offer morning service in a room at a neighbouring farmhouse which had been sanctified for the purpose. From the farmer's wife he could claim two eggs for his breakfast, a penny loaf, and half a pint of small beer, and hay for his horse.

Ynys Cwyfan has its 'legend'. It was said that one day a local family decided to picnic on the island. In the party was the family nurse. During the visit, she meandered into the graveyard on her own – this was before a wall had been built around it to prevent erosion – and she came across a damaged grave where the skull had rolled out of the crumbled soil. She picked it up and a loose tooth dropped into her hand. She slipped it into her pocket, intending to keep it. As she returned to the party she began to suffer from severe toothache which worsened as the day progressed and made her feel ill. Her employer noticed her discomfort and the nurse told her of her experience in the graveyard. Her employer ordered her to return the tooth to the grave, which she did, and gradually her toothache disappeared.

St Cwyfan's church atop its rocky island

St Cwyfan's church

Golden sands at Ynys Feirig

A wild sea around Ynysoedd y Gwylanod at Rhoscolyn

Of such tales are legends born.

The reefs and rocks around this coast have been a danger to shipping over the centuries, especially in the days of sail, and at a time when there were no coastal charts. The seabed is littered with shipwrecks. More of these later, but one should be mentioned here.

The clipper 'Norman Court' was on a return passage to her home port, Liverpool in 1883. A violent storm blew her off course towards the coast. She sent a distress signal. Two of the crew died after a night spent clinging to the rigging. The Caergybi (Holyhead) lifeboat made two unsuccessful attempts to reach her to save the rest of the crew. The attempt of the Rhosneigr lifeboat, too, was unsuccessful as they were unable to launch their boat. But the Holyhead crew were not to be deterred. They hired a train to take them within sight of the ship, make their way across the moor to the shore and managed to launch the Rhosneigr boat. What had appeared to be a hopeless task was completed. The Holyead lifeboat crew received medals from the RNLI for their bravery and determination.

During the 18th and early 19th centuries the Crigyll Robbers were active. They were local farmers whose cattle roamed the shoreline fields. On dark, stormy nights the farmers would tie lamps around the necks of their cattle and when these moving lights were seen from unsuspecting ships out in the bay the captains would believe that there they would find a safe berth. Only when it was too late their cargoes were seized.

Court records at Beaumaris refer to cases where charges were made and some of the Crigyll Robbers received prison sentences.

Today, all is quiet on Ynys Cwyfan.

A new church was built on the mainland, opposite the island, and this, too, was dedicated to 'saint' Cwyfan.

Holy Island (Ynys Cybi) from the air

Ynys Cybi (Holy Island)

Anglesey's largest off-shore island, Ynys Cybi, lies off its north western point, jutting into the Irish Sea. It is separated from mainland Anglesey by a narrow channel known locally as The Inland Sea.

Before Thomas Telford built his London to Holyhead road now called the unromantic name, A5, Ynys Cybi was reached by crossing The Inland Sea over the 16th century stone bridge of Pontrhydybont, or Four Mile bridge as it is close to the fourth milestone from Caergybi.

This road is still used by travellers to Rhoscolyn and Trearddur. Today, however, there are three more options – Telford's A5, the railway, and the modern expressway A55.

Geographically, Ynys Cybi has something of everything. Land on the edge of The Inland Sea is marshy. Behind Rhoscolyn and Trearddur there is farmland. Westwards it becomes rocky, culminating in the great, steep cliffs of Ynys Lawd and Ynys Arw (South and North Stacks) backed by Mynydd Caergybi (Holyhead Mountain) before falling again to the flatter land around Caergybi itself.

Tourism is the main industry today. The inner harbour at Caergybi is a natural creek, developed to meet the changing demands of shipping and trade.

The town has seen times of decline, then prosperity, then decline again. In the early years of this century the vast Anglesey Aluminium plant at Penrhos ceased operation, leaving many without employment, but plans are afoot to regenerate the area with a difference, so maybe there will, once again, be an upsurge in its fortunes.

So, what does Ynys Cybi have to offer us today? After crossing Four Mile bridge, a quiet lane leads to Rhoscolyn, passing a worked out stone quarry. This was bought by George Bullock, a Liverpool cabinet maker of repute. He recognised the potential of this uniquely marked purple, green and black stone as a decorative feature he could use in the heavy pieces of furniture so appreciated by his wealthy clients.

Plas Rhianfa, a mansion on the road between Porthaethwy and Beaumaris, has a fireplace surround decorated with Mona Green Marble, as the stone was called. And the then government commissioned him to make a very large table for the house at Elba which was the 'prison' of Napoleon Buonaparte at the time. Liverpudlians remember George Bullock for another reason – he was the founder of the Liverpool Academy.

Ynys Cybi is scattered with ancient monuments – standing stones, an important burial chamber, forts and hut circles, and a Roman wall.

The cliff pathway along the south side of the island has a small stone memorial, inscribed 'Tyger'. Tyger was a dog who was shipwrecked with his master, another man and a boy. Although it was a foggy night, Tyger's instinct was unerred, and he swam, leading his small party, to the shore where he licked his master's hand, and died.

Trearddur was once called Towyn y Capel, but when it developed as a resort the name changed, picking up the name of a local farm.

Shipwrecks along this coast happened often.

Even the advent of steam power was no match for one of these, when the four masted screw barque SS Missouri

Winter sunset over Ynys Lawd (South Stack)

The suspension bridge giving access to Ynys Lawd (South Stack)

Building of South Stack lighthouse

A south westerly gale creates a stormy seascape

hit rocks one stormy night on her way to Liverpool with a mixed cargo of live cattle, palm oil, hides and bales of cotton. She hit the rocks at Porth Dafarch, and sent a distress signal which was picked up by a lifeboat station. In an attempt to lighten the load, the crew drove one quarter of the hundred and fifty cattle overoard. But to no avail.

A lifeboat saved twenty of the crew and some stowaways, but the remainder of the crew stayed on board to await the arrival of a tug to attempt to pull the ship off the rocks. This was unsuccessful, and explosives were used which broke the ship into pieces, which sank beneath the waves.

Ferocious weather could make it difficult, sometimes impossible to berth vessels at Caergybi's inner harbour and it was decided to create a second berth on the sheltered side of the island, to be used in such circumstances. This was at Porth Dafarch. But the idea was short lived as steam powered boats came to be used and these found no problem. The landing stage at Porth Dafarch, and the road cut through the rock to enable passengers and goods to have access and egress, can still be seen.

Since the reign of Charles II in the 17th century appeals had been made for navigational aids around Ynys Cybi. It was not until the late 18th century that permission was given for a light to be placed on Ynys Lawd (South Stack), and the first light shone in 1809.

Imagine the problems facing contractors on such a site. The cliff opposite Ynys Lawd fell vertically down to a sea which was always turbulent. There was no landing place on the island for materials, equipment and workers. So four hundred steps were cut into the cliff side, and a hemp rope slung across the chasm from which a large basket was suspended so that it could slide along, this large enough to carry men and materials. And so the deed was done.

The lighthouse is not manned these days, but automated from the Trinity House centre at Harwich.

Visitors are allowed, on a regulated ticket system, but all are warned that not only must four hundred steps be negotiated on the way down, but these have to be climbed on the return, too. After the light began to operate, the number of shipwrecks decreased dramatically.

Overlooking Ynys Lawd stands a conspicuous tower. It is Ellin's Tower, built during the 1890s by William Owen Stanley, a wealthy landowner, as a retreat for his wife, Ellin. Today it is used as an information centre by the RSPB where thousands of visitors arrive each year to watch through binoculars as seabirds jostle for space on the cliff ledges opposite, to nest in the spring and raise their young. It is one of the most popular visitor attractions on Anglesey.

A huge cave a little further along is called Parliament House Cave. Thousands of birds arrive here, too, to nest and make such a noise that it is well named.

A pathway leads to North Stack where there is a fog signal, and where there are, too, remains of the semaphore telegraph station, the first in a line between here and Bidston Hill on the Wirral and Liverpool. Coded signals were received here from ships entering Liverpool Bay on their way to deposit cargoes at the Liverpool docks, an early warning system for merchants who could prepare in advance for a quick turnaround. Operators at the signal stations could manipulate the heavy signal arms from

Ynys Arw (North Stack) fog signal station

The remains of Holyhead to Liverpool Telegraph Station overlooking Holyhead harbour

Llyn Llwynog, created for the country park

A full moon rises above standing stones at Penrhosfeilw

within the signalmen's houses and they became so adept that messages could be passed along the coast, given favourable weather, in a matter of minutes.

From the summit of Mynydd Caergybi (Holyhead Mountain) one has an extensive view of the town and the harbour. The great Breakwater catches the eye, stretching to enclose the new harbour. One can appreciate the immensity of the project. Salt island, at the entrance to the inner and original harbour, has seen many uses. Customs dues were collected here, at one time there was a factory extracting salt from sea water, and there was a sailors' hospital.

A plan to enlarge harbour facilities across Newry beach was submitted by engineer J. M. Rendel and adopted. The breakwater of over one mile was to be built from Soldiers Point – ending in a lighthouse. Stone for the base of the breakwater was quarried on Mynydd Caergybi and carried down by rail to Soldiers Point. A large workforce was needed, so there was work for many local people and many Irish 'immigrants' whose presence in the town brought a new atmosphere. As a result this was a time of comparative prosperity for Holyhead but it brought its problems, too, as Caergybi lost some of its Welshness and became known more widely as Holyhead. And there were social problems, too.

Rendel planned a square lighthouse to mark the end of the breakwater as he believed this would make it easier for the keeper to furnish.

Today the new harbour is filled with small craft, leaving the original inner harbour free for ferries and merchant ships.

Tŷ Mawr hut group

Eglwys Llan y Bedd and St Cybi's church

They Came to Live in Caergybi

Every town has its residents who have contributed to its development and character, and Caergybi is no exception.

Several have been outstanding in the world of literature, music, publishing or religious matters. The four chosen to be remembered here had very wide interests.

William Morris was an Anglesey man though not born in Caergybi. He came to the town on his appointment as excise officer in the port. This was in the 1730s. He lived there until his death thirty years later. He was one of the famous Morris brothers who wrote scores of letters to each other. Letters which give today's historians such a vivid picture of life in Anglesey at the time.

William was a man of many talents, a musician, a botanist, a keen gardener and interested in medicine and surgery.

When he arrived to work in Caergybi his brother Lewis also worked in the port, but left later for mid Wales. It was Lewis who charted the coast of Wales, invaluable information for sailors.

William settled in his new environment and this was made easy through a friendship with another newcomer, the Rev. Thomas Ellis.

Thomas Elis was a Flintshire man. He had been sent to Caergybi by Jesus College, Oxford, to be curate in charge of St Cybi's parish church. He was a man of strong character, ideally suited to make some of the sweeping changes necessary which he believed would improve the standing of the church in a population which appeared to have little

47

respect for it. William, with others, agreed. Thomas Ellis also sought to improve living conditions in the town.

He was fond of children. He set up a school for a few of them at the small building near the entrance to St Cybi's churchyard, Eglwys y Bedd. He also supported the circulatory schools system active in his day. Thomas Ellis' interest in education was remembered in later years when one of the town's primary schools was named after him.

In what spare time the two friends had, they created a garden near to where they lived.

Up on the hill Morawelon, overlooing the harbour stands a huge memorial which catches the eye of everyone approaching the town, whether by rail, road or sea. This remembers John MacGregor Skinner, another 18th century resident. Skinner was born in America, the son of the King's Attorney General to New Jersey. He served in the Navy where he lost an arm during the American War of Independence, having previously, as a child, lost one eye. On leaving the Navy, he joined the Post Office and was sent to Caergybi in charge of a packet boat on the Irish ferry service. While living in the town he too became interested in improving social conditions and was known for his generosity. He was also critical of the Post Office regarding the condition of their ships, which, he claimed were poorly constructed. The service was lacking in several respects, all hindering development.

One October night in 1832 his vessel encountered bad weather, and Skinner was swept overboard. His body was not recovered until some days later.

The inscription on the memorial, funded by friends,

J. MacGregor Skinner

Skinner monument on the Alltran Rock

Pontrhydybont (Four Mile Bridge)

Stanley chapel in St Cybi's church

The Stanley Embankment takes Telford's road into Holyhead

describes Skinner as 'distinguished for zeal, intrepidity and fidelity'. And, of course, his charity.

What better site could there be for the Skinner memorial than this, overlooking the harbour and the town in which he was so involved.

When Thomas Telford was building the last stages of his London to Holyhead road, he created what we now call the Stanley Embankment.

This took his road towards the town. It was so called because it passed over part of the Stanley estate at Penrhos.

Today there are many references to this name in Caergybi. They remind us of the generosity of this family who were so important in the town's development.

The Stanley family originated in Cheshire. One of its members married Margaret Owen of Penrhos, and they had two sons. One of these, William Owen Stanley, was to become such a significant character in Caergybi. The Penrhos estate was large and employed many local people in the grounds and in the house.

William Owen Stanley was a man of several interests, a painter, archeologist, and interested in the social conditions in Caergybi. The Stanley family provided the town's water supply, a market hall, and a sailors hospital on Salt island. On the day of his funeral, the town came to a standstill, with people lining the streets to pay their last respects as the cortege wound its way slowly to St Cybi's church, where William Owen Stanley was buried.

His tomb of Carrera marble, flanked by large angels, is visited by many even today.

Ancient Monuments on Ynys Cybi

Ynys Cybi (Holy Island) is rich in ancient monuments, some of which are in public guardianship. These date from the Neolithic Age to the Roman occupation.

There are two standing stones at Penrhosfeilw, each ten feet tall, standing eleven feet apart. These stand sentinal close to Porth Dafarch. There is a smaller one at Tŷ Mawr, near to Trearddur. These date from the Neolithic period, 2600BC to 1900BC.

Trefignath burial chamber is about a mile and a half south of Caergybi. It is regarded as a fine example of a segmented chamber. It has a continuous passage, and was once divided into three or four chambers. At the end of the 18th century a number of stones were removed, to be used as gateposts locally. The burial chamber would, originally have been covered with an earth mound.

Hut circles were built within a fort, usually on high ground. There are remains on Mynydd Caergybi and Mynydd y Twr. Those on Cae'r Twr, close to Ynys Lawd, are of uncertain age. Hut circles on Mynydd Caergybi date from the second to the fourth centuries AD.

The remains of twenty hut circles can be seen here, circular with a central fireplace and one rectangular one.

The wall surrounding St Cybi's churchyard in Caergybi is of Roman origin. It was part of a small fort overlooking the harbour, a three sided edifice which allowed the Romans a clear view of any approaching marauders.

After the Romans left Anglesey, and 'Saint' Cybi arrived, he was allowed by Prince Maelgwn Gwynedd to establish his cell within those walls. His cell, in time, became a monastery where Cybi would welcome followers, and later where the parish church was built.

The wall is a thick construction of mortared rubble, covered with stones set in a herringbone pattern. It is regarded as one of the finest Roman walls in Britain.

There are other ancient monuments on some of the other islands around Anglesey, notably Ynys Llanddwyn and Ynys Seiriol.

Trefignath Burial Chamber

The Past Passes into the Future in Caergybi

For centuries Caergybi has been a port with special associations with Ireland. This from the days of sail to steam powered vessels and the more sophisticated ships of today. Caergybi has its maritime museum to mark these changes.

The Museum was founded some years ago by an enthusiastic group of residents, most of whom had connections with the sea. They collected artefacts which were housed in premises in the town, but those enthusiasts longed for a place nearer to the sea. Their dreams came true when the old Holyhead Lifeboat station house became vacant. So everything was moved to the building at one end of Newry beach. The Museum had come home. What better place than one of the earliest lifeboat houses in Wales. This, in itself, was a piece of maritime history.

Today, the artefacts are well displayed in a pleasant gallery. There is a shop where books and memorabilia are sold, a cafe-bistro overlooking the sea with an extension actually built out over the water, and in the old Second World War air raid shelter by the Museum entrance there is an interesting collection of items concerning Holyhead during the Second World War.

The Maritime Museum in Caergybi is certainly taking the past into the future as the enthusiastic volunteers look forward to welcoming many visitors during the years ahead.

The building of the Holyhead Breakwater was a

mammoth task. It was one which the town was proud to achieve at the time, and intends that the story should not be forgotten.

Stone for the base of the Breakwater was quarried from Mynydd Caergybi (Holyhead Mountain) and taken down to Soldiers Point by rail. The Breakwater would snake away almost three miles into the bay, nearly enclosing Newry beach, the end to have a lighthouse.

After the work was completed and the quarries closed, the area remained derelict for some time until someone, somewhere, had a vision. Why not convert it into a country park, where its story could be told for future generations in pleasant surroundings?

Landscaping began, a small lake was made, the remains of the silica brickworks incorporated in the design, and

The breakwater in Holyhead harbour

there would be an information centre where those interested could learn about the Breakwater project – and enjoy a cup of tea.

The Breakwater Country Park is an attraction which deserves to be well known, this is yet another example of Caergybi taking its past into the future.

High above the town, in the area appropriately known as Ucheldre, stands a tall, shapely tower, the chapel tower of a convent school which once stood there.

Mention has already been made of the ups and downs of Caergybi's economy over the years. As the last century came to an end, the upkeep of the school was becoming a burden and it was decided to close. The school was demolished to make way for housing, but the chapel and its tower remained. What use could be made of this architectural gem?

Now, thanks to the vision of a number of local residents, it is the hub of the Ucheldre Arts Centre. The intention was, and continues to be, that the Centre should reflect 'the arts' in their widest form. Not only is it the venue for singers, instrumentalists, actors, with world-wide popularity, but it is also equally important that here is a stage for all manner of local, amateur, arts activity. There is an exhibition gallery, local societies of all kinds meet here. This is a busy place.

Success does not come easily, which the founders well know. Constant hard work is necessary if such a place is to be successful, as the Ucheldre Arts Centre truly is.

Caergybi will take its good intentions into the future here.

The Skerries

The more well known name for Ynys y Moelrhoniaid (the island of seals) is The Skerries, believed to be a Norse name describing the rocks which lie to the north of Carmel Head.

These rocks are important to navigators, as they mark the entrance to Liverpool Bay. They are especially dangerous to those who pass by too closely and have been the cause of many a shipwreck.

Today, a lighthouse gives due warning of the danger. This was the first lighthouse to be built on the Welsh coast.

Two flashes of light every ten seconds can be seen across twenty two nautical miles, given the appropriate weather conditions.

The lighthouse is distinctive in daytime by one broad band painted horizontally around its 23m tower. The Skerries also has a fog signal which gives two blasts every twenty seconds.

A lighthouse on the Skerries was proposed as far back as 1639 by a private speculator who had an eye on the financial benefits if he could charge tolls on passing ships, but the proposal was not allowed as it was then thought to be an impossible project. Another attempt was made in 1705 which was also opposed.

The entrepreneurial spirit was not easily doused. By 1713 an Irishman, William Trench, had obtained a sixty years' lease from the owner of the island. The following year the government gave Trench a patent for a beacon, allowing him to levy dues of 'one penny per ton on all shipping benefitting from the light except our ships of war'.

The first light, coal fired in an iron basket, appeared in 1717. It was only after the first boatload of workers were lost in a wreck that this happened. It was a tragic beginning to the venture.

Trench later paid a Crown rent of £5 a year and had the right to levy one penny per ship and twopence per ton of cargo. The expense to keep the beacon lit outweighed his assets. Although he began the project a wealthy man, he soon lost considerably. When he died in 1729 he had many debts.

The beacon and all those debts passed to his wife and family, and it was his son in law, the Rev. Sutton Morgan, who handled the business on their behalf.

An Act of Parliament allowed him to increase the dues and confirmed the patent. Until then the leaseholder of the Skerries could only levy the same tolls on both British and foreign ships, whereas lighthouse owners elsewhere had more beneficial terms.

The Skerries lighthouse had to have keepers, and William Trench had employed a couple, husband and wife, to live in a cottage he had built for them on the island. It was the keeper's responsibility to feed the beacon with coal – between eighty and a hundred tons a year were used. This method of lighting had its drawbacks, of course, as its efficiency depended on the weather.

The story goes that the keeper's wife opened her cottage door one windy night, to find a coloured face peering at her in the dark. He was a shipwrecked sailor seeking refuge. It was probably her first experience of a coloured man, and must have come as a shock to her.

When the owner of the Skerries died, his grandson paid

The Skerries lighthouse

The Skerries lighthouse stands on the middle island of three

occasional visits. One of those visits ended in tragedy when he and twelve friends returning from the island, were wrecked and drowned. This northern coast of Anglesey, in the days of sail, saw many wrecks. Mention of some of these is in the next chapter.

A contemporary sketch of 1740 shows the iron basket sitting on the top of a stone tower about thirty to forty feet tall, surrounded by a parapet.

By 1759 Morgan's heirs had rebuilt the tower at a cost of around £3,000. In 1804 the top was raised and an iron balcony with railings added.

The top was glazed and a cupola positioned. It was looking more like the lighthouse we see today.

By this time the port of Liverpool was growing fast and shipping along the north coast of Anglesey was busy.

The Skerries could be a profitable asset, one which the lessees wanted to maintain. During the 19th century, when Trinity House was seeking to take over British lighthouses, five years after an Act empowered them to purchase, the lessees of the Skerries had stubbornly refused to sell on several occasions, a court was convened in Beaumaris. Dues paid had reached the astronomical figure of £23,000 a year. The jury at the court awarded the heirs of the property £444,984, a sum which Trinity House could ill afford to pay, but pay they did. And so the Skerries passed into their hands.

After purchase Trinity House commissioned architect and engineer James Walker to restore the lighthouse. He was articled to his uncle in London. The company was involved in designing twenty lighthouses around Britain.

The Skerries gave Walker the opportunity to design a

stylish group of buildings including a keeper's cottage in an attractive court yard.

Today there is no longer a keeper in residence, as the light is automated through Trinity House's centre at Harwich. Their representatives visit regularly to maintain the lighthouse, arriving by helicopter, landing on a specially constructed helipad.

One feature of the Skerries rocks has not changed. The turbulent seas around them can be as dangerous as ever they were in Trench's day.

More Shipwrecks around the Island

Storms, the rugged coastline to the west and north of Anglesey, with treacherous sandbanks to the east and south, have all contributed to the number of shipwrecks over the years.

One of the most famous took place close to the Skerries in the 17th century.

When Charles II was crowned, his brother in law, William of Orange who had married Charles' sister Mary, made him the gift of a large yacht, named after the lady. But 'Mary' was too large to be used in the Thames, so was put into service conveying passengers of importance to and from Ireland.

In March 1675, close to the Skerries, 'Mary', the first royal yacht, was wrecked. She capsized and her mainmast touched the shore, allowing thirty nine passengers and crew to scramble ashore. The yacht broke up immediately, and the captain, bosun and thirty other passengers drowned.

A chance dive by members of a Lancashire sub aqua club in more recent years found two bronze guns from the 'Mary'. This prompted further search, and numerous artefacts were found, including silver and china and even a female skeleton. These were taken to the Maritime Museum at Liverpool for safe keeping.

The eastern entrance to the Menai Strait, at Ynys Seiriol, (Puffin Island) has a large area of submerged sandbank the Lavan Sands. This is an area which has proved to be hazardous to shipping in foul weather.

In 1831, 'Rothsay Castle', an early steamer, sailed from Liverpool for north Wales. She was known to be unseaworthy but was still in service. The skills of her captain and crew left much to be desired.

As the ship left the Mersey, the weather deteriorated. The passengers pleaded with the captain to return, but to no avail. As conditions in Liverpool Bay worsened, they pleaded again, but were refused. The captain was adamant that all would be well. After a long delay, the ship struck a sandbank on the Dutchman's Bank on the Lavan sands. She sheered off, but struck again, and this time the mainmast and the funnel fell, killing the captain and his mate. A local boat attempted a rescue, but only twenty passengers were saved out of one hundred and fifty.

Following this tragedy, a petition pleaded for a lighthouse overlooking the narrow channel between Penmon and Ynys Seiriol. This was provided. The Trwyn Du light has a range of twelve nautical miles.

The western entrance to the Menai Strait has also seen shipwrecks. This is the site of Caernarfon Bar, well known to sailors. It is overlooked by the lighthouse on the southern tip of Llanddwyn island.

Around 1840 the full rigged sailing ship 'Mountaineer' was on her way to deliver a cargo to Liverpool when she was wrecked near Caernarfon Bar. She broke up, and wreckage was strewn along the Llanddwyn shore. One of the pieces, a ship's figurehead, was picked up by a naval man living near Caernarfon, who took it home and mounted it as a feature in the house.

The crew of 'Mountaineer' were saved, except for one boy who was caught in the rigging, and drowned.

There is a rock off Ynys Llanddwyn called 'Craig y Mochyn'. This reminds us of a wreck which took place nearby. The steamer 'Monk' was carrying a large cargo of live pigs. All the crew, and the pigs, perished in the wreck hence the name of the island. It is said that pork was on the menu of cottagers living on Llanddwyn for a long time after the incident.

Malltraeth Bay to the north of Ynys Llanddwyn has seen wrecks, too. Locally based lifeboats made some brave efforts to save life, but not always successfully. This happened at a time when lifeboats were large rowing boats, manned by eight oars craft which were also vulnerable in bad weather.

The 'Soane went aground here, and asked for help. The lifeboat prepared to give assistance, but was driven ashore, and the oars were lost.

A message was sent to Tal y Foel where there was a boat truck, and a team of horses dragged it to where the lifeboat had beached. The boat was lifted on to the truck. The team then made post haste to a spot near to the endangered ship, new oars were provided and the lifeboat was safely launched. The crew of the 'Soane' was saved, and later the ship was relaunched.

In 1892 the clipper ship 'Primrose Hill' was wrecked on the north coast of Ynys Cybi. Thirty three lives were lost. The ship was outward bound from Liverpool to Australia. She was caught in a north westerly gale off Ynys Lawd (South Stack). In spite of attempts by more than one lifeboat to save her, it was useless. One member of the crew did manage to save himself, as he was on the rigging and jumped ashore from there.

In 1908 the steamship 'Harold' was wrecked between the two Stacks, and it took the Caergybi lifeboat four hours to cover the distance of five miles between the lifeboat station and the ship. The crew of the 'Harold' was saved and taken to Caergybi but the ship remained fast on the rocks, and eventually broke up.

This is only a brief mention of some of the many wrecks which have happened around Anglesey's islands. There are many more stories of tragedy and bravery.

The Islands' Lifeboat Stations

Two hundred years ago there were no lifeboat stations on Anglesey. A life saving service was needed urgently to combat the lack of navigational aids around the coast. The provision of such a service was thanks to the persistence of a newly married couple, James and Frances Williams, who, in 1821, came to live on Anglesey, he as rector of Llanfairyngnghornwy and she as rector's wife.

Shortly after they arrived, James Williams took his wife down to the coast for a walk. It was a wild day. They saw a ship in distress – the packet boat 'Alert' – and while they watched, she holed and began to sink. They gazed, horrified and helpless. There and then, they decided to work to provide a life saving service. All 'Alert's' one hundred and forty passengers and crew were lost in the wreck.

James Williams financed the first lifeboat himself, a large rowing boat, and this was kept at Cemlyn. Being an accomplished sailor, he was its coxswain. The couple persuaded their more wealthy friends and neighbours to contribute towards the cost of the new venture which was called the Association for the Preservation of Life from Shipwreck, the intention being to set up several lifeboat stations around Anglesey, several on its islands. This was in 1828. Frances Williams made her contribution to the effort by painting, and selling her pictures.

These lifeboat stations were responsible for saving very many lives. In due course the Association was absorbed by the RNLI which has responsibility for them today.

At present there are lifeboat stations at Trearddur and

Caergybi, but in the days of sail they were also at Rhoscolyn, Llanddwyn and Porth Rhuffydd.

Navigational aids began to appear, too. On Ynys Llanddwyn provision began early in the 19th century, when there was brisk coastal trade in and out of Caernarfon and the Menai Strait. A pilotage system was set up to guide ships over Caernarfon Bar. This was at a time when the incidence of shipwrecks was high. Admiral Crawley, who lived outside Caernarfon, was perturbed about the lack, as was James Williams, and he financed the first boat to be stationed on Ynys Llanddwyn. This, in 1828, was to be manned by the pilots. His gift was made through the Anglesey Association. But although his intention was good, it created problems as there was no slipway or boathouse and manning the boat on demand was sometimes impossible as the pilots could be busy on their piloting. This part of the island was so sparsely populated and crews could not be found.

The boat was then moved over to Caernarfon but this, too, was unsatisfactory, so the Caernarfon Harbour Trust built a slipway and boathouse in a more convenient position close to the beacon which was a landmark into the port. A small cannon was provided for the Llanddwyn pilot which was placed outside his cottage. If a distress call was received, this was fired to alert a crew living in Newborough who then had to make their way as quickly as possible to launch the lifeboat. Even with this difficult procedure a considerable number of lives were saved before the Llanddwyn lifeboat station closed in 1907. The closure came about through better facilities being made available at other stations on the islands.

The SS Missouri shipwreck at Porthdafarch on 1st March, 1886

18th century view of St Cybi Church and Holyhead town

Holyhead lifeboat: Christopher Pearce

A memorial to Jof Rogers who swam ashore with a lifeline during the Royal Charter shipwreck at Moelfre

The cannon still stands outside the pilot's cottage, however. It, too, has a story. When H.R.H. the Prince of Wales was undergoing helicopter training at RAF Valley, as part of his final test he had to lift a piece of equipment and carry it to the airfield. So the cannon had an air-lift. It remained on the airfield until public protest demanded its return to Ynys Llanddwyn.

Rhoscolyn was believed to be an ideal location for a lifeboat station, from where aid could be given to ships in distress to the south of Ynys Cybi and as far south as Llanddwyn. The rocks and reefs there were a constant danger. The station was opened in 1830 with a boat provided by the Anglesey Association. This, of course, was a large rowing boat and a crew was found to manipulate its eight oars. A boathouse was built at the expense of Hampton Lewis of Bodior, a large house nearby.

The Rhoscolyn station had an excellent track record, and worked in conjunction with lifeboats at Caergybi and Porth Rhuffydd when needed, before it, too closed.

The courage and bravery of these crews over the years is legendary. So many lives were saved, and many awards and presentations made in recognition.

Boats have been renewed over the years, reflecting changes and improvements which make handling them easier.

As the village of Trearddur began to develop as a resort, a new demand for the help of the lifeboatmen emerged. A station was provided here. Accidents to holidaymakers on the water have to be addressed, as well as distress calls from ships in trouble during a storm.

The Trearddur lifeboat centre today has staunch

support from residents and visitors. Volunteers give time to help at the shop and welcome many visitors during the tourist season.

One might expect to find a lifeboat station at Caergybi. This station is one of three oldest along the coast. In 1821 a committee was set up to consider a station here. Lloyds of London were approached to finance the building of a boat and offered £50, but there is no record of this having been accepted. Not until 1828 was a boat delivered, the cost of £80 being met by the Anglesey Association. There is a model of this in the Maritime Museum at Caergybi.

During its first one hundred and seventy five years of service, the Caergybi lifeboat saved over one thousand lives at sea.

On occasions, the islands' lifeboats have worked together when the need has arisen, and they will continue to do so.

Islands along the North and East Coast

Looking out to sea from Carmel Head (Trwyn y Gadair), one sees the small island of Maen y Bugail (Rock of the Shepherd) otherwise known as West Mouse. This lies east of the Skerries. This coast has many small islets, sometimes no more than sharp rocks standing clear of the water.

Harry Furlong's rocks are an example. Who was he? Harry was a local man who placed a beacon on the rocks following a shipwreck. This was replaced by Trinity House later by a green conical buoy. Harry's real name was Furlough – but the rocks lie a furlong off shore.

Middle Mouse is off shore at Cemaes. The Welsh name, Ynys Badrig, celebrates the Irish Saint Patrick who was shipwrecked here. He was fortunate to reach dry land on the coast where he raised his cell, and later a church was built on the holy site, giving us Llanbadrig. This is one of the oldest churches in Wales.

East Mouse (Ynys Amlwch) is at the entrance to Amlwch port. It must have witnessed great activity at the time when copper was exported from the port.

There is one small island on the east coast. This is where sandy bays proliferate so Ynys Dulas, in Dulas bay, stands out. The tower on the island was built by a landowner who lived at Plas Dulas. It was intended as a refuge for any shipwrecked sailors before they could reach the safety of the mainland. A lady of the manor saw to it that food and drink was usually available here.

The last time the tower was used was during the Second World War, when the crew of an aircraft which had come

Ynys Badrig (Middle Mouse)

Llanbadrig's church with the island in the distance

down in the bay reached it – although, by then, the generous lady of the manor had passed away.

Ynys Seiriol
(Priestholm or Puffin Island)

Ynys Seiriol is a hump of limestone a mile long, lying only a very short distance from Penmon, on mainland Anglesey. Access can be difficult, due to turbulent water and tidal flow. The channel is very narrow.

After visiting Ynys Seiriol during the latter half of the 16th century, William Worcester in 'Itinerarium' describes it as being 'separated from the mainland as by the distance covered by the flight of two arrows with bow shots' and records seeing its surface 'covered with elder trees'. He found rabbits and adders there.

There was once a great colony of puffins, hence the English name, but a count in 1990 revealed only thirty pairs. That same count also revealed four hundred cormorants breeding – over half the Welsh cormorant population. There was also a colony of kittiwakes.

When puffins were abundant, they were caught and pickled packed in barrels and sent to the cities where they were considered a delicacy. Then a persistent colony of brown rats searching for eggs among nesting seabirds, has been blamed for the decrease in numbers.

Grey seals sometimes rest on the foreshore of the island. They are an attraction to tourists who take the occasional boat trip from Beaumaris to see them.

The effect of myxamatosis prevalent through Britain in 1954/5 changed the pattern of plant life on Ynys Seiriol because of absence of rabbits.

An early religious settlement, founded by 'Saint' Seiriol

in the 7th century became a monastery and later a church. The monastery was of the Augustinian order. It is not known how many were in that early settlement. Burials took place there, as graves have been found. Seiriol's original sanctuary became the monastery church. Its tower remains.

When the semaphore signal system, mentioned in a previous chapter, was set up to carry maritime messages from Caergybi to the Liverpool warehouses, a station was sited on Ynys Seiriol. Signals were relayed from here to the Orme at Llandudno, then along the line to the Wirral. The system ceased to be used when modern telegraphic techniques came into popularity, and the building was taken over by the Liverpool Marine Biology Committee and used as a laboratry. This was later moved to the Isle of Man, but the remains of the building on the island remind us of its previous uses.

Ynys Seiriol has always been regarded as a mystical place. Legends telling us of lands below the sea have always been a part of folklore.

The Lavan Sands, just off the coast, have their tales to tell. At very low tide, 'walls' are seen protruding which, for centuries, have been regarded as part of a lost city. But scientists say they are merely accumulations of stone left from the Ice Age. So much for imagination.

They wrote about Anglesey's Islands

One of the earliest travellers to Anglesey to record his impressions was Giraldus Cambrensis (Gerallt Gymro, Gerald of Wales). He accompanied Archbishop Baldwin during the 12th century to preach and to whip up enthusiasm for the Crusades. He left posterity an account of this tour in his 'Itinerary through Wales'. He visited Ynys Seiriol which was then, he wrote 'inhabited by hermits who lived by manual labour and served God'.

It was he who recorded the legend of small mice who lived on the island, appearing if the hermits had a disagreement and passions were raised. They would raid the food store. But as soon as the disagreement was resolved, they would disappear.

During the 18th century Ynys Seiriol had another visitor – Thomas Pennant, the naturalist and antiquarian. Pennant, too, was travelling through Wales, and his 'Tours in Wales' describes with enthusiasm, the puffins he found on the island, and the plants which interested him.

In 1784 Pennant also wrote of the plants that interested him on his visit to Llanddwyn island. This place, he said, was covered with sand dunes. He reminded his readers that during the reign of Henry VIII the church on Llanddwyn was the richest in the Bangor diocese. This came about, he decided, through the large number of pilgrims who visited St Dwynwen's well, and left offerings at the church in gratitude for help in alleviating their afflictions.

The ferries from Caergybi to Dublin prompted several to write of their experiences – some complimentary, others not. In today's services of fast ferries, they make interesting reading.

Roderick O'Flanagan, in 'Through North Wales with my wife' wrote of the passage from Ireland to Caergybi on a fine day, the pleasant sail, and the warmth of the welcome they received at Caergybi.

Dr Jonathan Swift's experiences of the crossing and of Caergybi were very different. And he did not mince words. He complained of the weather which kept the ship in port, the behaviour of the crew, and the disgusting accommodation he endured while waiting to sail. All this in his diary.

After the Menai Strait had been spanned by Telford's Suspension bridge, diarist Francis Kilvert, who had been staying in Bangor, went along to see it. He walked along the new road out of Porthaethwy, enjoying the views as he went, and met an old man who was ready to talk to a stranger.

'How would you like to live in that house, summer and winter, all the year round?' asked the old man, pointing to Ynys Gorad Goch. 'They live like fighting cocks there, they have a weir and catch all the fish.'

But local writer David Senogles, whose book 'Ynys Gorad Goch' was published in the 1960s, thought otherwise. He wrote of the hardships endured by the families living on the island before many of today's facilities were available.

This is but a sample of the very many who have visited and written of their experiences, some of them when access was difficult. How different it is today, when visitors can arrive by road, rail, sea or air, and take life on Anglesey very much for granted.

Will any of this year's visitors decide to write of their experiences for posterity? Now, there's a challenge!

Further Reading . . .

Anglesey Antiquarian Society Transactions – various
The Welsh Academy Encyclopedia
Anglesey and the North Wales Coast: F. H. Glazebrook
A Guide to Ancient Monuments on Anglesey: CADW
Faster than the Wind, Liverpool to Holyhead Telegraph:
    Frank Large
Holyhead, the story of a port: D. Lloyd Hughes and
    Dorothy M. Williams
Hard Men, hard stone, hard bricks: John Gareth Roberts
Mynydd Twr, Holyhead Mountain: Edwin Roland Owens
The Holyhead Breakwater and Quarries: Edwin Roland
    Owens
Prehistoric Anglesey: Frances Lynch
For Want of Schooling: Eryl Wyn Rowlands
Ships and Seamen of Anglesey: Aled Eames
*The Ancestry, Life and Times of Commander John
Macgregor Skinner:* Peter Scott Roberts
The closed lifeboat stations of Anglesey: Jeff Morris
Wreck and Rescue on the coast of Wales: Henry Parry
Ynys Lawd, Goleudy South Stack: Ian Jones
The story of Ynys Gorad Goch: David Senogles
Anglesey, a concise history: David A. Pretty
Holyhead, people, prosperity, poverty: John Rowlands
Môn, Mam Cymru: Philip Steele and Robert Williams
The Ucheldre Centre: David Crystal
Anglesey Lighthouses and Lifeboats: Margaret Hughes